Laws of Investing

By Marcus Gram

Foreword by John Joyner

Our Company

In 2019, Adrian Kennedy began publishing books for independent authors from his office in Charlotte, North Carolina. His goal was to provide authors with more options and control over the publishing process at prices anyone could afford.

Today, the family owned and operated, Xscape Publishing company still continues to honor the founder's tradition of providing high-quality products and valuable services to the community.

First published by Xscape Publishing 2021

Copyright © 2021 Marcus Gram

ISBN 978-1-956799-02-6

All rights reserved. No part of this book may be reproduced or transmitted in any form or by any means, electronic or mechanical, including photocopying, recording or by any information storage and retrieval system, without written permission from the author.

Marcus Gram asserts the moral right to be identified as the author of this work.

Marcus Gram has no responsibility for the persistence or accuracy of URLs for external or third-party Internet Websites referred to in this publication and does not guarantee that any content on such Websites is, or will remain, accurate or appropriate. Designations used by companies to distinguish their products are often claimed as trademarks. All brand names and product names used in this book and on its cover are trade names, service marks, trademarks and registered trademarks of their respective owners. The publishers and the book are not associated with any product or vendor mentioned in this book.

None of the companies referenced within the book have endorsed the book

First edition

LIMIT OF LIABILITY/DISCLAIMER OF WARRANTY: THE AUTHOR MAKES NO REPRESENTATIONS OR WARRANTIES WITH RESPECT TO THE ACCURACY OR COMPLETENESS OF THE CONTENTS OF THIS WORK AND SPECIFICALLY DISCLAIM ALL WARRANTIES, INCLUDING WITHOUT LIMITATION WARRANTIES OF FITNESS FOR A PARTICULAR PURPOSE. NO WARRANTY MAY BE CREATED OR EXTENDED BY SALES OR PROMOTIONAL MATERIALS. THE ADVICE AND STRATEGIES CONTAINED HEREIN MAY NOT BE SUITABLE FOR EVERY SITUATION. THIS WORK IS SOLD WITH THE UNDERSTANDING THAT THE AUTHOR IS NOT ENGAGED IN RENDERING LEGAL, ACCOUNTING, OR OTHER PROFESSIONAL SERVICES. IF PROFESSIONAL ASSISTANCE IS REQUIRED, THE SERVICES OF A COMPETENT PROFESSIONAL PERSON SHOULD BE SOUGHT. NEITHER THE PUBLISHER NOR THE AUTHOR SHALL BE LIABLE FOR DAMAGES ARISING HEREFROM. THE FACT THAT AN ORGANIZATION OR WEBSITE IS REFERRED TO IN THIS WORK AS A CITATION AND/OR A POTENTIAL SOURCE OF FURTHER INFORMATION DOES NOT MEAN THAT THE AUTHOR ENDORSES THE INFORMATION THE ORGANIZATION OR WEBSITE MAY PROVIDE OR RECOMMENDATIONS IT MAY MAKE. FURTHER, READERS SHOULD BE AWARE THAT INTERNET WEBSITES LISTED IN THIS WORK MAY HAVE CHANGED OR DISAPPEARED BETWEEN WHEN THIS WORK WAS WRITTEN AND WHEN IT IS READ.

TABLE OF CONTENTS

INTRODUCTION 1

FOREWORD 3

Chapter 1. STACK YOUR MONEY 5

Chapter 2. ACQUIRE ASSETS 15

Chapter 3. DON'T POCKET WATCH 25

Chapter 4. FLEX WHEN NECESSARY 34

Chapter 5. ACT YOUR WAGE 44

ACKNOWLEDGEMENTS 52

Laws of Investing
By Marcus Gram

Introduction

I started writing this book two years ago. I didn't officially start writing it two years ago, but it was two years in the making. It's similar to when you hear an artist say they've been writing their first album their whole life. I didn't write this book to tell you how to become a millionaire. Hell, I'm not even a millionaire myself. About 95% of Americans won't ever become millionaires. That's why it was important for me to write this book. I've seen plenty of millionaires write books once they're millionaires telling you how to do it. I thought it was better to write this while I'm working towards that goal. Sometimes we see millionaires and think we can't ever become one. I mean, up until last year, I'd never met a millionaire, especially not someone who was around the same age as me. I damn sure never met a millionaire who wasn't an athlete or entertainer. What's important for me is to allow people to watch my journey. To see the success in real-time and be inspired. I want people to look at me and not see how easy it is to obtain but see and know that they can obtain it. I want people to see that I'm not special. Everything that I'm doing, they can do. I want people to say to themselves, "if he can do it, I know I can too." I went from making $30,000 in 2018, to $70,000 in 2019 and to over $230,000 in 2020. I never dreamed that I would earn $230,000 in one year, especially before 30. When I moved to Philadelphia in 2018, I just wanted to live better than I was currently living. I didn't care if my dreams seemed far-fetched or unrealistic. I wanted to make a change at all costs. I can't tell you how to become successful. What I can tell you is how I've found success and hope that you can take something from that and use it to help you find success. I hope this book shows you how much you are really in control of your life.

Foreword
By John Joyner

As a black man growing up in South Carolina in the Jim Crow era, I was the son of sharecroppers. We were broke and didn't have anything. When I was 16 years old, I told my parents I wasn't working as a sharecropper anymore. We worked every day from sun up to sun down and never had anything to show for it. Somehow, we always ended up owing or breaking even with the field owners. They convinced us that giving us food and shelter was enough payment. Everyone accepted that because that's the way things were. They always believed that God would make things better or fix everything. But it never made sense to me. So, I had to do something different. I got my first job not soon after at the cotton gin making $.045 an hour. Having that job showed me what money does to transform your life. It showed me how people perceive you and how you're accepted in society when you're making money. I went from being the outsider to the insider. We're conditioned to think being poor is acceptable. You hear the saying, "money isn't everything." Well, money isn't everything when on its own, but it can provide you with everything you need. People who are broke and don't have money operate out of fear for much of their lives. Money gives you options that aren't afforded to people who don't have any. It provides you access to things and people that wouldn't be available to you if you didn't have it. One thing I've always told my grandson was that it's not about how much money you make; it's about what you do with it. If you're making $1,000 a month and spending $1,000 a month, you're broke. You have to put some money to the side for a rainy day or to make investments. I tried teaching this to all of my kids and grandkids, but my grandson was the only one who was receptive to it. He always asked questions and was inquisitive. So, while I'm happy to see him try to apply it to his life, I'm not shocked by it. Thank you, grandson, for allowing me to share everything I know with you. I'm proud of you.

Chapter 1

Stack Your Money

"Great achievement is usually born of great sacrifice, and is never the result of selfishness."

-Napoleon Hill

What do you want to achieve, and what are you willing to do to achieve it? You want to get in shape, but are you willing to dedicate your time to working out and eating healthy? You want to be a professional athlete? Well, are you willing to work on your game for hours every single day? There's no reward without sacrifice. In September of 2016, my then-girlfriend and I moved into a very nice townhome in the suburbs of Rochester, NY. We'd both finished college a year earlier. I completed graduate school, obtaining my master's in developmental disabilities while she completed her undergraduate degree in communications. Before moving into this townhouse, we stayed in a small one-bedroom apartment about 20 minutes away. This was a spot that we moved into to move out of my mother's attic. The new townhouse was amazing to us. We had two bedrooms, a washer and dryer, a patio, a bathroom in our room, pretty much everything we wanted at ages 25 and 23 years old. I thought we were living! During this time, I started to take an interest in real estate. My grandfather had a lot of experience in real estate, owning about 10 homes at one point in his life. He always talked to our family about the importance of ownership and purchasing real estate. Unfortunately, most of my family had no interest. This was due to them hating what they called "preaching" from him. While everyone loved grandad and appreciated his advice or occasional loan, no one wanted to hear the speeches that came with it. I was different. The speeches motivated me. But nothing motivated me more than seeing this huge house he had built in his hometown in South Carolina. You see, my grandfather moved to Rochester, NY, from Charleston, South Carolina, when he was 17 years old. He spent most of his life up until that point working as a sharecropper. He was only able to attend school when it rained, and the fields were shut down. Being a sharecropper was normal for everyone around him, but he always thought bigger; he always wanted more. So, at 17, he moved up North for a better life. Now because he could only attend school when it rained, he did not know how to read or write when he relocated. My grandfather did not learn how to read or write until he was 21. He landed a job at General Motors, and because of his work ethic, they wanted to see him succeed in life, so they paid for him to attend night school. So, here I am at 25, looking at this amazing house that my grandfather, who worked years without making a single dime, who could not read or write until he was 21 years old, had built. Boy, was I motivated. I was sold. That was the day I officially became his student. From that day forward, I spoke to my grandfather at least once a week about business. We would converse about family and life, but we focused a lot on business. The one thing that he routinely told me was to save my money. If I wanted to follow in his footsteps, I would need to make some sacrifices. I was ready to start. There was just one problem. I was not in the position to save any money. Let alone enough to purchase real estate. Remember, my girlfriend and I were recent college graduates. I worked as an assistant manager at a residential home for people with disabilities, and she worked at a call center. We both were earning about $15 an hour at our respective jobs. Not to mention I had a son. With our new townhouse, a new car for me, paying different credit cards, etc., we would've been lucky to save $200 a month. So, I made an executive decision to downgrade where we lived to save money. Luckily the property management where we lived allowed us to transfer to a cheaper apartment they owned. Instead of two bedrooms, we only got a one-bedroom apartment. While everything was going according to plan, my relationship wasn't doing so well, so we split with her keeping the apartment. I originally planned to move into my one-bedroom apartment to try to save money. But a conversation with my mother changed it all. She was home alone and missed me a lot with me being away at college for most of the previous five years, and she thought it would be a good idea to build a great relationship. While I missed being around my mother too, I didn't like how it looked. I went away to college, came back home, started working entry-level jobs, had a failed relationship, and moved back home with my mother. I felt disappointed for a moment, but then I thought about the plan I had. I wanted to save money to buy real estate to grow a large portfolio and live the life I wanted. My will to succeed and create generational wealth for my family outweighed my ego. So, I decided to move in with my mother. To be honest, it was the best decision I ever made. I stayed there for nine months, and during this time, I was able to save $10,000. My mother owned her house, so all she required was help with the utilities and groceries, which was easy. Not paying rent helped me save a lot, but it wasn't just that. It was the mindset shift that I had. I decided to stop buying unnecessary things. I stopped ordering out, stopped buying alcohol, didn't go out to clubs or bars, and just bought the things I needed. Well, almost all the things that I needed. Having a child meant celebrating holidays and birthdays, so of course, I had those spending obligations. However, when celebrating his birthday and other holidays, I made sure to buy things for him and not for me. When I say that, I mean that many parents throw big parties or buy all of these crazy expensive gifts for their kids, and the kids don't even care for it. It's all a show to impress other people. They want to show the world how they "ball out" for their kids. So many times, those same people have trouble covering their bills after spending all of that money. Now I'm not here to tell you not to celebrate holidays with your kids or buy them nice gifts. No, that is not what I'm saying at all. I'm just talking about this being one of the many ways that people spend unnecessarily. Were there times I wanted to buy something expensive? Absolutely. Did I want to go out with some of my friends? Of course. But the more I started to save, the less I felt pressured to do those things. When I talk about sacrifice, I'm not just speaking about monetary things. There's a big chance you'll have to sacrifice relationships. As much as we would like to have everyone come with us on our journey, it's not likely to happen. Some people won't see your vision, and you have to understand that is okay. I come from poverty. It takes people seeing it to believe it. Don't take it personally that a friend or family doesn't immediately see what you see. Don't hold a grudge. Execute your plan and show them. More times than not, they will follow once they see it's a reality. While I was saving my money, I most certainly had family ask me to borrow money. Over and over, I told them, "No, I don't have it. I gotta save for this house I'm trying to buy." Did some people think I was acting funny? You damn right they thought that. But did I care? Well, I did. I really wanted to help my family. I wanted to help them a lot. It's not easy seeing your family struggle. As I said before, I was living in poverty.

Everyone around me was living in poverty. Even with that said, I was still making the most money out of all of us. Ain't that some shit? I'm making around $15 an hour and felt the burden of looking out for my family at times. Now here I am with $10,000 in my bank account, watching people around me struggle while I constantly tell them that I can't help them. I felt horrible, but I knew that if I could invest this money, I would be able to help my family long-term. So, if you guys are reading this, I'm sorry, but I did what I had to do for us. Living with my mother was great. Saving money aside, I enjoyed the time we spent building a very strong relationship. I always had a knack for being distant and standoffish, so while we loved each other, we never had the mother/son relationship we had hoped for. The time we spent living together pretty much made up for all that. We lived like roommates. We respected each other's space and boundaries. We were able to address any issues that would arise, and most of all, we just talked. My mother had just turned 50, and she had her dreams and aspirations that I was always happy to hear about. She was always down to listen to the many dreams that I had. I probably talked to her about a million different ways that I was going to be a millionaire. Bless her heart for listening each time. Now, I have $10,000 in my bank account. I'm ready to buy a property; my sacrifice is over! Not exactly. By this time, I had decided to move to Philadelphia. I had a college friend out there looking to get into real estate, and he thought it would be smart to engage in group economics. I, initially, was hesitant because although I was so ready to move out of my hometown, Philadelphia wasn't exactly in my top 25 places to live. It was five hours away from home, and if I were to move, I wanted to move somewhere warm. Philadelphia is not a place you would consider warm to live. But I did feel that I'd outgrown my city, and my dreams were much bigger than my small city could provide me. That and I'd either quit or get fired from every job in the industry in which I worked. My current job was literally the last in the city where I could work in the human services field. I originally planned to move to Philadelphia in September of 2018. But in the spur of the moment, I made a life-altering decision. On the day before Valentine's Day of 2018, I walked into my boss's office and quit. I decided to do that because I knew that if I waited seven months to move to Philadelphia, I wasn't going to move. I would've gotten too comfortable and stayed. So, I couldn't give myself something to fall back on. I couldn't give myself any time to be talked out of my decision. I had to go. My girlfriend and I had rekindled our relationship, so she agreed to move with me. The move benefitted her because she's originally from Brooklyn, NY, which is only about 2 hours away from Philadelphia. On February 15th, 2018, I said my goodbyes to my family and moved to Philadelphia. Now some people think moving in with my mother was the ultimate sacrifice. Hell no! Moving in with my friends in Philadelphia was the ultimate sacrifice. My friends were a married couple with three kids. We stayed in their daughter's room on a twin-sized bed. I'm 6'1 and weigh over 200 pounds. A twin-sized bed for me is small on my own. Now you add another human being to that bed, and we're talking about suffocation. But we made it work. Living with my mother was easy. Yes, there were times where she forgot I was an adult, but there was still a level of comfort there because my mother's house was home. This was different. It wasn't bad, just different. I imagine that's what it's like for professional athletes to join a winning team and not try to step on anyone's toes. The team has a winning formula, and you just don't want to mess that up. It took a lot of time to adjust. I also had to adjust to living with my girlfriend again. Prior to moving to Philadelphia, we had lived apart for almost a year. While adjusting to living with our friends and their family, we were also working on our relationship and getting used to being in each other's space again. There were moments I wanted to move back home. Moments might be selling it short. There were weeks and months I was ready to move back home. Regardless of how comfortable they tried to make us feel, we always felt like guests there. Not only was that difficult, but I was battling depression. I'd dealt with depression before but nothing compared to this. I missed my son a lot. I didn't feel comfortable where I was living, and I started to feel like I had made a big mistake moving in the first place. I promised my girlfriend all of this success that I was going to have, and yet here we are, sleeping in a 7-year-old girl's bed. What really helped me during this time was the conversations that I would have with my mother. Every day she would call me and provide positive affirmations. She encouraged me to repeat these phrases every day; "I am successful, I am important, and I am somebody great." She believed that if I looked in the mirror every day and said these things, I would start to believe it. If I started to believe it, then I would regularly act on them. To this day, I say those phrases. Words can't express how much those conversations meant to me. As difficult as everything seemed, I couldn't bring myself to give up. This was the sacrifice that I needed to make to achieve my goals and dreams. I had to keep pushing. My son, girlfriend, and family depended on me. So, after taking a suggestion from my friend about putting some money into owning vending machines, I invested $7,000 of the $10,000 that I had saved while living with my mother. To be honest, I only needed to invest about half of that. I entered a vending machine program that was a complete waste of money. I won't say the program's name, but I will tell everyone that you do not need to invest thousands of dollars into any vending machine program. It's simply not worth it. But you live, and you learn. It would take me about two months before I bought my first vending machines and placed them in a business. After all of the sacrifice, it seemed like I was really on my way to becoming the successful man I had dreamed I would become. Regardless of the struggles, I will always appreciate my then friends for opening up their homes to us. While life has taken us in different directions, many of the opportunities that have come my way in Philadelphia can be traced back to them, allowing my girlfriend and me to move in with them. So, to the Edwards family, thank you.

Chapter 2

Acquire Assets

"If you do not find a way to make money in your sleep, then you will work until you die."

-Warren Buffet

First, let me say this, everyone does not have to be a business owner or entrepreneur. Working a traditional 9-5, 2-10, or an overnight shift for most of your life is 100% fine. Most businesses cannot survive without employees. Employees are essential for businesses. So, I'd again like to reiterate that everyone does not have to be a business owner or entrepreneur. But everyone should be an investor. Having more than one source of income is pretty much a must nowadays. With the cost of living continuing to rise but salaries not increasing to match that, the average person may find it difficult to live the life they want with only one income. When I started investing in the vending machine business, it was supposed to be a "side hustle" for me. My goal when moving to Philadelphia was to find success in real estate. My friend and I talked a lot about group economics. For those of you who don't know what that is, that's where you put money together with a group of people who share a common interest and use that money to purchase or invest in something that each person stands to benefit from. We thought it would be better for a handful of us to put up $5,000 to purchase a $20,000 property versus one person looking to save $20,000 to purchase a property on their own. While I was down for group economics, everyone didn't have their money yet, so my friend suggested that I get a couple of vending machines. Once I have those machines, I could save those profits and use them towards the property I would eventually invest in. This was the first time I'd be investing in anything, so I was extremely excited but slightly nervous. I mean, I had $10,000, and I don't care what anyone says on Twitter, that is a lot of money. There were so many things that I could do with that money other than planting it in an investment that I couldn't guarantee would work. When you're living in poverty, you almost have no room for error. Even with that in mind, I was willing to go all in. My thought process was simple, I've lived in poverty my whole life, so if this fails, I'll be right back where I was before. But if it works, then I get to change my life, and my family lives better forever. It was a no-brainer for me. Now, of the $10,000 I had saved, $2,000 had to pay bills back home for my girlfriend and me. I kept $1,000 for personal spending and put $7,000 to the side for the vending machine business. As I previously said, I entered into a vending machine program. That program was supposed to teach me the game, help me with my branding, and find vending machine placements. I paid $2,800 for this program, and I was severely underwhelmed by it. But I was new to the game, and there was a hard lesson I learned from the experience. If you look like a sucker, you will get licked. Even though I was disappointed with the money I spent on the program, I was still very excited. I was starting my own business. Seeing my logo and my name on my business cards gave me a sense of pride that I hadn't felt in a while. With all that said, I needed a job, badly. While I did invest $7,000 into the vending machine business, as I originally said, I didn't invest $7,000 all at once. My decision to put aside $1,000 for personal spending wasn't a smart idea. Thinking about it right now, I have no idea why I thought that would work. I had a girlfriend and a kid. There was no way I could just live off $1,000 for however long it took for my business to get up and running. So, I had to use some of the money I was saving for the vending machine business to get by. I had $4,000-4,500 to my name. That may sound like a good amount, but it goes by so fast when you don't have any money coming in. I'm in a new city, and even though I started working on my business right away, I still had to experience the city. So, we're going out to places, and since I'm a guy who believes his woman shouldn't have to pay for anything, my money was going out rather quickly. I started looking for jobs, and because of my work in the human services industry, it didn't take long for me to find a job. I landed a job as a residential manager at a group home. My goal at that job was to use the money I made to continue to fund my vending machine business. Unfortunately, that lasted three weeks. After two weeks of training and one week of working on-site, I walked off in the middle of my shift. The house was having issues, and I was supposed to get things under control. One week of dysfunction, and I concluded I could not manage someone else's company when I have my own company. Now I didn't have a single vending machine business when I quit, but I truly believed that my business would be big one day. From that point on, I started working long enough to complete the training phase and quit once I received my first check. I did that for at least three jobs. I decided I would only work a job that required minimal responsibility from me. I eventually found a job that was perfect for me. I became a one-to-one behavior specialist for an adult with autism in his home. The job was created by his family, who, let us say, have "old money". Their family founded one of the biggest colleges in America. The only hint I'll give you is that their college basketball athletes are known for getting injured when entering the NBA. Now the reason I chose this job was that I didn't have any co-workers, no real supervisor other than the client's mother, the hours were 3-10 Monday-Friday which would allow me to work on my vending business during the day, and it would be the most money I ever made at a job. During this time, $42,000 a year sounded like a lot of money to me. It was a lot better than the

$27,000-30,000 a year I was used to making. The only thing better than getting this job was that I placed my vending machines the same day I was offered the job. It only took me a month and a half to find my first vending machine location. I was more proud of this moment than any of my college graduations. I placed two vending machines in a business office just right outside of Philadelphia. I felt so accomplished at that moment. I was a business owner. This one location was the first step in my million-dollar dream. After placing the machines, my friends and I popped champagne for the accomplishment. The celebration was short-lived because the location was nowhere near as good as I thought it would be (that's something we'll get into later). At this point, things were becoming a little more stable. I liked my job not because it was such a great job, but because it was an easy job and let me work on my business and my future while there. I worked at this job for almost a year. For the entirety of the time I was there, I would plan my whole life. Every day, I would write on a piece of paper my one-year, two-year, and three-year goals. The goals were always income-based. I wanted to make $90,000 in year one, $100,000 in year two, and $125,000 in year three. Every day I would adjust the numbers. Now just saying I wanted to make that amount of money meant nothing at all. If you ask the average person what they would like to accomplish, they'll say they want to be a millionaire. Most have no plan on how to accomplish that.

So, underneath each income goal, I'd write how I planned to achieve that. I figured the easiest thing to do would be to specialize in something to earn top dollar. That'll be my foundation for investing. I already had a master's in developmental disabilities, so I wanted to expand on that. I noticed in Pennsylvania that autism was a big deal, so I decided to enter a post-graduate program on Applied Behavior Analysis at Drexel University. Many who complete that and go on to become board certified are able to earn up to more than $100 an hour. If I could make that amount of money, I'd be able to buy more vending machines and start purchasing real estate property. That foundation was key to me. I've seen so many social media "gurus" tell people to quit their job and go all-in on their dreams. They'll tell you that while you're working a 9-5, you're helping someone else's dream come true. Being an entrepreneur and business owner is difficult. It's very difficult. It takes so many people a while to even break even, let alone make a profit. My first vending location took me months to start making any money. Not profit. I meant it took me months to make money. I'm overexaggerating a little bit, but the amount of money I was making versus the amount I spent to start up was pennies. I would have been in such a poor spot if I didn't work because I wasn't going to make anyone else's dreams come true. You need money to make money. That is something that'll never change. Even with all of my current success, I still work. I currently work as an independent contract behavior consultant. I make $90,000-$100,000 a year doing that. That job pays my bills and allows me to invest in more vending machines, which allowed me to invest in a home healthcare business that I now own, which allowed me to invest in the stock market. Having that foundation puts me in the position to keep reinvesting my profits. While my job is my foundation, my investments are what allow me to be financially free. Investing in vending machines saved me from what could've been a very dark time. In April 2019, I was fired from my job. I wasn't necessarily surprised by it. I wasn't able to complete the job I was hired to do because of my clients' health concerns. So, I spent a lot of time doing nothing on the job. While I wasn't shocked, I also wasn't prepared. I didn't have another job lined up. I had just entered this post-graduate program, I needed this job to complete my clinical hours, and I was 15 days away from moving out of my friend's house into an apartment with my girlfriend. Did I also mention we were a few weeks away from having a baby? Even though all of that was true, surprisingly, I wasn't upset or concerned about losing my job. Hell, I was kind of relieved. I know it sounds crazy but being fired motivated me to take control of my own life. I hated the thought of someone dictating whether I could take some time off or even pay my bills. I mean, I did all I could at that job, and one day they just let me go. I didn't get any kind of two weeks' notice. I was motivated to make moves for myself. I saw a few postings for independent behavior consultant positions and applied to them. With that position, you are self-employed. You don't have a boss or any co-workers. You pretty much make your schedule. I was sold; this was exactly the type of work I needed. The pay would be by far the most money I'd ever made. I was confident I'd get a contract with at least one of the agencies. So, I was in good spirits. Instead of sulking, I took the next couple of weeks off to play basketball which is my first love. I've played for over 20 years. During this time, I was currently rehabbing a fracture in my right knee. I had just finished my last physical therapy session the day I was fired from my job and was ready to get back to playing. While I'd love to tell you that I enjoyed this time of working on my business, playing basketball, and just not having to wake up to go to work, that wouldn't be true. In fact, the worst thing that could've happened to me happened. Four weeks after getting fired from my job and finishing physical therapy, I tore my ACL in my left knee. Well, simply saying I tore my ACL is an understatement. I tore my ACL, meniscus, patellar tendon, quad and fractured my femur. I cried when I got the results from my MRI. I cried to my girlfriend, and then I cried to my mother. I felt like my life was about to take a turn for the worst. I just lost my job, I'm back in school, I just got a new apartment, and I have a baby on the way. How the hell am I supposed to take care of all of those things if I couldn't even walk? I just signed a contract as a behavior consultant. Why would they want to move forward with someone who can't walk for three to four weeks? Not to mention the work I was looking to get involved with involved people with aggressive behaviors. For a moment, I feared being homeless. I may have gotten through two sentences before my mother interjected and said, "stop that, you're thinking of all the worst things that could happen instead of focusing on the good things that will happen." When I moved to Philadelphia, I was extremely depressed. Not being able to see my son every day and just the circumstances of my living situation plus the stress of trying to be successful overwhelmed me. However, I was able to turn to my mother during that time for support, and she always came through. Before ending each conversation, she would always say the serenity prayer to me, "God grant me the serenity to accept the things I cannot change, courage to change the things I can, and the wisdom to know the difference." I'm a big overthinker, so when my thoughts begin to impact me, I think of this prayer. My mother suggested to me that maybe I had gotten complacent with my job, being that up until that point, it was the most money I'd ever made, and the job was pretty easy. She felt that maybe I needed this time to sit down and refocus. My oldest son was coming up the following month to stay for the summer, and I had a son on the way. Maybe I needed this time to spend with my family and be there for my girlfriend, who will need my support after having the baby. When I listened to my mother explain this, I got very optimistic. It did seem like I had gotten stagnant. While by that time I acquired four more vending machines, I wasn't actively working on my business. I was going through the motions. I did need to focus, and at the same time, I could spend the summer having fun with my family. I was motivated. What motivated me most was paying my bills because of the money I'd saved from my vending machines. While the emotional and mental support I got from my loved ones during this time was huge, I still had to pay the bills, and I wouldn't have been able to do that without my business. What started as a side hustle literally saved me from not being able to pay my bills. That is what made me feel strongly about telling people to invest. You have to have some sort of extra income coming in. While a job is said to be your safety net, you can't forget that at any moment, it can be taken away from you. You're not given a heads up to get your affairs in order. They will fire you with no hesitation. So, invest in something. There are a ton of things you can invest in while maintaining a job. You can invest in vending machines, real estate, the stock market, or the crypto market. Hell, I've seen people invest in trading cards. There are many other things I'm leaving out, but you can research ways to make money and find what works for you. The chances of you being as successful as you want to be are reduced if you

Chapter 3
Don't Pocket Watch

"Comparison is the thief of joy."
-Theodore Roosevelt

Lack of focus plays a major part in some people not achieving success. Many people say they want to be successful and may even start the process of working towards it. But along the way, they get distracted for various reasons. To be honest, it happens to all of us. No one is exempt from lack of focus. But to get to where you're trying to go, you're going to have to get back on track and become extremely focused. You just don't want to focus on the wrong things. Focusing on what you don't have compared to your peers will almost surely prevent you from achieving success. I've seen so many people between the ages of 30 and 35 see someone 21 years old having financial success and begin to get discouraged because they feel they're so far behind. Those kinds of thoughts stop people from even trying to achieve their goals. They start to feel like it's never going to happen for them, which isn't true. When I placed my first two vending machines in a location on May 4th, 2018, I was on cloud nine. I always knew I wanted to be a business owner. There were so many days and nights I dreamed about it. To have it come true just seemed surreal to me. However, as I previously said, I barely made any money at this location. It was mostly my fault. I didn't assess the location as well as I should have. I assumed there were triple the number of people in the location than there were. In hindsight, what I would've done differently would've been getting a combo vending machine (half snack and half drink) as opposed to one full-size snack machine and one full-size drink machine. The first few months of having the vending machines were brutal. I averaged about $60 in sales a month between the two machines. I probably lost about 500 dollars during that time due to some of my products expiring. Shit, at this point, I wasn't even looking to make any profit. I was hoping to make my money back. The first week was nerve-wracking. I was constantly checking my sales reports to see if I had made any money. I didn't make any sales until the third day of my machines being in the location. There was a big sigh of relief when I checked the report and saw a sale for $1.60. That sigh of relief was followed by excitement. I know that you're probably laughing at me for being excited over a sale of $1.60. But it wasn't the amount of the sale. It was the fact that there was a sale in the first place. You see, that sale did nothing but prove that I could make money with vending machines. Maybe this location wasn't going to earn me much, but that didn't mean there wasn't a location for me out there that would. All I needed was for me to see that I could make money doing this. I just needed the visual. So, instead of being discouraged, I took care of those machines like they were making me $6,000 a month instead of $60 a month. I came out weekly even though I didn't need to, responded to service calls promptly, and built relationships with the staff. I wanted to be as polished as I could be for when I obtained some great locations. Now during this time, my friend was in the vending machine business and doing well. He was making a few thousand dollars a month from his machines. Did I care? No. Not one bit. He had more experience than me. He'd put in a lot of work, so it made sense. Even when he told me his first location earned him $900 a month, which is a lot more than $60 a month, it didn't discourage me. In fact, it motivated me. All I heard was the potential amount of money that I could make off a machine or two. Hearing someone talk about their success has always motivated me. While some people have a 'why them and not me?' mentality, I've always had the mentality of "if you can do it, I can do it." I've never thought that in a comparison kind of way. It came from the mindset that if that person achieved it, then it can be done. Why can't I do it? Even though I had a long way to go to make money from my business, I knew that my time would come. I didn't worry about my friend making more money than me. Instead, I focused on finding ways to increase my vending machine sales. With some help from my friend, I found a strategy to boost my sales. What's one thing that no one will ever turn down? No, not that. Free money! Everyone loves free money. So, to increase my sales, I'd buy a handful of scratch-offs and place them on the back of some of my snacks. What that would do is create buzz around the location. Someone would buy a bag of chips and find a free scratch-off on the back. They would then buy more snacks, hoping to find another scratch-off, and then tell their peers in the location about it. This was something I would do once a month. I used this trick until I ultimately took the machines out two years later. By the time I severed ties with the location, it was generating $200-250 a month in sales. I started to build up my vending machine route slowly. Five months after securing my first vending machine location, I offered a deal to buy a vending route. A vending route is vending vending machine location, I offered a deal to buy a vending route. A vending route is vending machines already placed in locations making money. So, you skip over the hard part of finding locations. Think of it as when you buy an investment property and a tenant is already living in the property. You don't have to do the hard part of looking for a tenant, and you start making your money back right away. A route consists of two or more locations. So, when you're buying a vending route, you're essentially buying someone's vending business or a part of it. The vending route offered was 15 vending machines placed in various settings from the banks to colleges. The sellers wanted $7,000 for the route. To be transparent, I didn't have anywhere near that amount of money. So, I partnered with my current business partner, who wanted to get into the vending machine business and went half on the purchase price. I took eight machines, and he took seven. This was it. The hard work paid off. I was going to start making some good money with my vending business. Unfortunately, that was not the case. While I did sell four of my machines for $2,500 because the driving distance to service them was too far, the other four machines were not bringing me much money at all. Surprisingly I wasn't disappointed. I guess going through it before helped me deal with it. I mean, I wanted to make more money, but I had a sense of pride in owning my own business, and I knew it would turn around. While my locations weren't doing too well, my partner hit the ground running with his locations. All of them were doing pretty well. While some would've been disappointed and wished they had chosen the other machines, I was happy for him. I was happy that he didn't have to go through what I had to go through with my locations. His success did not hinder me, and it did not make me jealous nor make me feel like everyone can make money with this business but me. I again was motivated and seeing the locations he obtained helped me identify what could potentially be a good location in the future. So, over the next year, I proudly serviced all six of the vending machines that I had. Each month they made more and more money. I wished the amount was more, but the extra money that

I was making with my business helped out a lot. I spent the summer of 2019 nursing my surgically repaired knee and spending time with my family. During this time, I wasn't looking for vending machine locations or promoting my website. I had a few good potential locations contact me. I had an apartment location with 200 plus apartments contact me for my services. When I scheduled this meeting, I knew this was my big break. 200 plus apartments meant I could make thousands of dollars a month off of my machines. I was very prepared for the meeting. I honestly knocked the meeting out of the park. The manager of the building loved everything that I presented and everything that I said. After finishing, she let me know that they would be contacting me in three to five days to let me know they made a decision. I was confident. Extremely confident. I had waited for this opportunity since I started in the business and knew this was my time. Of course, I didn't get the location. I didn't know what was worse, being told they went in another direction or being told the manager of the apartments chose me but was overridden by her manager who wanted to go with a more established company. Either way, I was disappointed. It was the first time I got a little down when it came to my business. I had done well staying grounded and not expecting too much, but this was truly an opportunity I thought I had in the bag. I wasn't able to dwell too much on it because soon after that interview, I received an email from someone working in Joe Biden's campaign, and they were looking for vending services while they worked on the campaign over the next couple of years. Based on the number of people in the establishment working daily, this sounded like a great location. I wasn't able to meet with them in person, but I provided my proposal via email. I answered any questions and concerns they had and yet again wasn't chosen for the location. At this point, I just accepted this year I wasn't going to get any more locations. So, I just focused on enjoying the summer with my family. So, that's what I did. I went to a few beaches, traveled a little, and just had fun. My business, while not major, was doing fine. I had started my independent contractor behavior consultant job, so my finances were in order, so when it was time for me to get more locations, I would have the money to spend. Little did I know my big break was around the corner. Two weeks before taking my son back home to upstate New York so that he could start preschool, I got an email one night inquiring about my vending services. They expressed interest and informed me it was a student housing building with over 500 students. They were willing to meet right away. We set the meeting for the following day. A student housing building with more than 500 students seemed like a great location to me, but it seemed like a great location for someone else. I wasn't going to obtain this location. I've been down this road too many times before. I'd get excited, get all dressed up, and sell myself to someone who was just going to say no. I was over it, so I decided I wasn't going to the meeting. It was going to be a waste of time for me. My girlfriend was a very optimistic person, so she was dead set on "you should go because you never know." I felt like I did know because I was an expert in rejection. After mulling over it for a few hours, I decided to go to the meeting. I didn't want to ever get into the habit of not being professional. My name is my name. It's the one thing I will live and die with. The least I could do is show up to a 15-minute meeting. I did. Unlike my other meetings, I didn't have a great presentation or sell the hell out of my company. In fact, I didn't do a presentation at all. I don't even think I was there for five minutes. Upon arrival, the property manager asked me to sign the contract, asked about commission, showed me where the machines would go, and asked when the machines would be delivered. Before I knew it, the meeting was over. I was damn near speechless. I'd spent all this time going to places and putting my best foot forward in these meetings just to be told no, and here I am securing a big location without doing any kind of work. Isn't it funny how that happens sometimes? This location has gone on to become my biggest location to date. I had hoped that I would earn $900 a month in sales from this location. That turned out to be a big undersell. This location generates over $3,000 a month in sales! Most people don't believe that number when I tell them that. Hell, I couldn't believe it either. The first week of sales didn't have me on pace for $900 a month. So, I thought it would be another underwhelming location. So imagine my excitement at the end of the month after seeing I made $3,000 in sales. I called everyone in my circle to tell them. This was everything that I had been working towards. I moved to Philadelphia on a $30,000 a year salary, and now here I am on pace to earn $36,000 a year off of one vending machine location. While I was ecstatic, I wasn't surprised. I knew this moment was going to come. I didn't know the exact day, month, or even year, but I knew it was going to happen. Even my friend knew. We went out to celebrate getting this location, and he told me he was proud of me. Not just for getting the location but for never wavering. I never lost sight of my goals. I never gave up or complained. I held my head high and kept working. I could've gotten discouraged and given up when I saw how successful my friends were with their vending machine business, and mine wasn't doing well. Now, look at me. I landed the biggest location of the three of us. Having tunnel vision paid off. So, regardless of how bleak things may be, no matter how much success you see people having around you, stay in your lane. Don't look left, don't look right. Just look straight away at the goals you set for yourself.

Chapter 4

Flex When Necessary

"Life should not only be lived, it should be celebrated"
-Osho

If there's one word I wish we would remove from our vocabulary, it's humble. I hate the word humble. I haven't always hated the word. If you asked me two years ago to describe myself, I almost certainly would've used the word humble at some point. Many people describe themselves as humble or encourage people to remain humble. I don't believe most people know what the word humble means. Humble means "to have or show a modest or low estimate of one's own importance." Is this what people are encouraging you to be? Is that what you think of yourself? I don't think that of myself at all. In 2016, I met with the woman who ran the human resources department at my then job. I was applying for a new job within the company, so I had an interview with her. She and I had a really good relationship, so most of the time I'd stop by, we'd spend an hour just talking and catching up. I can't recall the full conversation, but I vividly remember her chastising me because I wasn't giving myself the credit she felt I deserved. I had a really good resume and many accomplishments. The job was mine for the taking. I just needed to own it. She told me that almost every day she meets with different black people who have the experience and qualifications, but they constantly downplay them. They downplay themselves. What has always stuck with me from that conversation was when she said, "stop being so damn humble, if you don't celebrate you who will?" Since then, I've adopted that mindset. I'm not going to wait for someone to celebrate my accomplishments. I'm going to celebrate them myself. If that comes off as cocky or arrogant, so be it. You should celebrate every single one of your wins if you can. Now, when celebrating your wins, don't forget you don't have to wait until you have a big win to celebrate. Celebrate those small wins. Those small wins add up to the big wins. They are just as important, if not more important. I learned this important lesson from my mother. Over the last few years, we've developed a relationship where we're best friends. I'm inspired by her daily. That wasn't always the case. In fact, I held a grudge against her for years. From the ages of 3-10, I didn't see my mother much due to her being a drug addict. It's been 27 years since she dropped my siblings and me off at a friend's house and didn't come back. After a few days, my grandmother came to pick us up. I always felt that if I had gone to live with my grandmother, my life would've been great. She lived in the suburbs, and I would've gone to a good school. We always had fun at her house playing with my cousins and brothers. For a while, I hated everyone who had a hand in me not living with my grandmother during this time. However, now looking back on it, I don't think I would be who I am today if I had gone to live with her. I know I wouldn't be who I am today if I did. So, I'm happy that I went to stay with my great-aunt Lou. While I loved Aunt Lou, during the seven years I lived with her, I hated every second of it. The first few days there, I just cried. I wanted to leave so badly. But I couldn't. It was either my little brother and I live with my Aunt Lou or be sent to foster care. My father was in prison for murder, and my grandmother had a job where she wouldn't be able to look after my younger brother and me. My two older brothers were in school, so they were a lot easier to manage. So, now I'm stuck with my aunt, who I didn't know at all. My Aunt Lou was in her late 60's and was from South Carolina. What is abuse now was just regular discipline that we received from her. I won't go into the details, but I will say it got brutal at times. As I said, I hated every second I stayed in that house. I wanted to be with my mother at all costs. There were some occasions where we'd spend the weekends at her house. As you can imagine, those weekends felt like I was in a fantasy world. We got to play with our other siblings and cousins, sometimes we went to the movies, and did I mention we got happy meals from McDonald's? Those two days with my mother to me were like being in prison for years and getting a few days out to do whatever you want. So, you can only imagine what it was like having to go back home. While those weekends with my mother were amazing, they didn't happen often. In fact, more times than not, she didn't show up. Those times stuck out more while I was school-aged. For one we rarely got new clothes. The only time we got new clothes was on Christmas when my grandmother bought them. Now let me tell you something, I hated those damn clothes. I'm six years old. I didn't want any sweaters. I wanted some action figure toys. I wanted some wrestling toys. I've grown up to realize how much I took that for granted because today I can barely find any of my shirts in my closet. So, grandma, if you're reading this, I would gladly take a sweater now. So, as I said, we didn't get any new clothes. Well, technically, they were new to us but old to someone else. On at least one Sunday out of the month, around 9 pm, my Aunt Lou would get us out of bed, pack that station wagon of hers, and head to the Salvation Army. The Salvation Army was closed, but people would drop off bags of clothes at the store's entrance. My aunt wanted to get those bags of clothes before the Salvation Army got a chance to take them in on Monday morning. Those clothes were horrible. I mean absolutely horrible. I knew because the kids at my school let me know every single day. As we all know, kids can be pretty mean, which meant I had to fight almost daily. You can only imagine how excited I was after leaving school on Friday afternoon, ready to see my mom for the weekend. I would sit at the table, anticipating her pulling in the driveway at any moment. She was coming at five o'clock, and I couldn't wait. Then six o'clock came. Damn, she's not here. Okay, she'll be here at seven o'clock. Still no show. I know eight o'clock was pushing it, but I would hold out hope. Still nothing, so I'd go to bed disappointed, but I didn't give up hope because we still had Saturday. Even spending just one day with my mother was worth it. Of course, she didn't show up on Saturday either. Each week this would happen, and each week I would still hold out hope. I used to tell my little brother things like, "mommy's coming, but she's a superhero, so she has to fight all the bad guys first." That's what I truly thought of my mother. She was my superhero. My world was crushed when I grew up and realized she wasn't a superhero. She, instead, was a drug addict. All the abuse, all the pain I endured, was due to her drug use. That realization hurt more when my Aunt Lou passed away due to lung cancer a year after, and I moved in with my mother. That woman loved my brother and me. She wasn't perfect, but she loved us the best way she knew how. Even when we lived with our mother, we would call and ask her to pick us up and take us somewhere, and she'd stop whatever she was doing to be there for us. To this day, I haven't been able to forgive myself for not saying thank you to her. The night before she passed, I saw her in the hospital while she was in a coma. I told her how much I loved her and thanked her for what she'd done for my brother and me. I've always wondered if she could hear me. I really hoped she could, and I hope she can hear me now. You may be wondering why I am sharing this? It's not to give you my life story but to provide you with context. Context of why I was humble. All of my experiences, my childhood made me very appreciative of any kind of success I'd have. I was so appreciative that I didn't want to lose it. I didn't want to be too excited or brag too much so that it would be taken away. That's like many people in the black community. Many of us have had so much go wrong that we are just appreciative when things go right. We know what it's like not to have, and we don't want to run the risk of giving up what we've earned by not being humble enough. My grandfather once told me that he worked 80 hours in one week before. When payday came, he went to pick up his check, and he was shocked and scared to see his check was $381. He was shocked because he'd never seen that much money before in his life, and he was scared to cash it because he wasn't sure he'd ever see that kind of money again. He was scared it would get taken away from him. Think about that, he busted his ass working 80 hours in a week for a paycheck that he rightfully earned, and he couldn't be excited or celebrate it because he was fearful it would be taken away from him. We have to do away with that mentality. You've earned the right to celebrate what you have or won. You will not lose it because you aren't humble. Be appreciative, not humble. Celebrate the wins, big or small. As I previously said, I learned the importance of celebrating my small wins from my mother. After years of fighting her drug addiction, she was clean, and we moved back in with her. I learned over time that she wasn't fully clean. She would have relapses that I wasn't privy to. March 2015 was when I first realized that she was using drugs again. I was hurt. Extremely hurt. My siblings and I sat down and talked with her. She talked about the stress she was going through and vowed not to do it again. To my knowledge, she was done. To me, she'd gone years without engaging in that habit, so I was sure it was a one-time thing. It wasn't until I was ready to move to Philadelphia that I found out that she'd not only been using drugs again, but all those years I thought she hadn't, she had. Don't get me wrong, she wasn't using them every day or even every year. But it occurred enough over time. After finding out she was using drugs again, we talked, I told her I wouldn't abandon her, and she again vowed to be done with it. Obviously, with addiction, it's not easy to stop after saying you will. So, she continued to use drugs until late March of 2018. I'd been in Philadelphia for one month and was having difficulty adjusting there. The last thing I wanted was anything going wrong at home. If you've made it this far in this book, you know that something always goes wrong in my life. One day at work, I got a call from my sister, which was a little weird since she doesn't call. She'll more than likely send a text if she needs to contact you. So, we're on the phone just catching up about life, and I hear my brothers in the background. I was confused about the fact that they were all hanging out at 10 am when they all had jobs. That's when she told me that my mother had been missing for three days. They found her car abandoned, and some random guy dropped off her cellphone. They waited to tell me because they knew how hard it was for me in Philadelphia and didn't want me to lose track of what I was trying to accomplish. The only reason they contacted me was to let me know that they were filing a missing person's report. At this moment, I hoped she was at least using drugs and not dead. To our luck, that was the case. She was found safe, but her addiction had gotten the best for her. I immediately flew home, and we held an intervention. There I let her know that all the times she'd relapsed over and over again, it was because she never really took steps to get clean. So, this time we needed her to go to rehab and take the necessary steps, or my siblings and I will have to walk away from her. We couldn't deal with the pain anymore. From that day forward, she's devoted herself to getting clean and staying clean. She recently celebrated three years of being drug-free. I couldn't be more proud of her. Three years is a major accomplishment. What I love is that while three years clean is a major accomplishment, I remember her celebrating three days clean and 30 days clean. She celebrated each one of those days because they were both milestones for her. She doesn't get to three years clean without getting to three days clean. She's in a group where while she was celebrating 30 days clean, someone was celebrating 15 years clean. Was her accomplishment less important? Not at all. My mother called me excited as hell on her 30th day of being drug-free. That person's 15 years clean doesn't take away from or negate my mother's milestone. That's one thing I want people to understand. When you're celebrating or "flexing," you're not taking anything away from anyone. People associate flexing with putting people down. No, flexing is being proud of your accomplishments. No one knows what it took for you to achieve what you've achieved. If you bought a new Rolex watch and want to flex for Instagram, do that. The world doesn't know that there was a time where you couldn't afford a watch. You put yourself through school, started at an entry-level job, worked your way up, and now earn a salary that allows you to buy that Rolex. You don't have to explain that to them either because your accomplishment is your accomplishment. As long as you're celebrating your win and not attacking anyone, don't feel bad about how anyone takes it. Yes, some people don't celebrate their accomplishments. They use them as tools to put other people down. We don't support that. I'm pro-flexing. I'm not pro-putting people down. Unless they tell me to be humble, and in those cases, I just flex on them.

Chapter 5

Act Your Wage

"Live below your means and within your needs"
-Suze Orman

What motivates you to be successful? Is it to create generational wealth for your family? Is it to pay off the debt you've accrued? Or is it so that you can purchase expensive things to show people you have money? For most people, it's a combination of the three. Most people would like to find success to take care of their family, and if that leads to generational wealth, that's even better. Most people also have debt. Student loan debt and credit card debt are two of the most common debts in America. Most people would also love to have money to buy expensive things that they couldn't always afford. Where someone can run into a problem is if they're buying expensive things solely for appearances. We've all heard the saying "trying to keep up with the Joneses." Falling into that habit will almost always bite you in the ass. I want to be clear that there is nothing wrong with buying yourself something nice. I believe you should do that kind of thing from time to time. Treat yourself to something nice. But do it within reason. Yes, you may need a new car, but does it have to be brand new? A car is a car. It doesn't matter what kind of car it is as long as you're using it to go to the money. That's always been my mindset. By the end of 2019, my business had grown a lot from where I started. Along with the big student housing location, I secured a couple of apartment building locations. I started making more money as an independent contractor behavior consultant. I was now making the most money I'd ever made. I expected to have success, but I didn't expect it to come that fast. I had my first $10,000 month in December of that year, and I can't lie, I was on the verge of tears. Just six months prior, I was worried about taking care of my home, and now here I am, having a five-figure month. It was so hard to explain. I tried to explain it time and again on the various podcasts I'd been on in the previous months, and I'm still not sure if I've done a good enough job. While I expected my success, I did not expect the attention that came with it. Somehow, someway I went viral on Twitter that September, which is still a mystery to me. At this time, I had about 90 followers, and of those 90, maybe four people interacted with me. So, late one night, I sent out a tweet stating I made $3,000 in sales from one vending machine location. Now I didn't think anyone would see my tweet. I tweeted about my business before, and no one seemed to care. I was tweeting this because I was so excited about this location. After sending the tweet, I went to bed. I had to be up early for work. When I woke up, I had a ton of notifications. I honestly had no idea what was going on, but I started to engage with any and everyone who began to ask me about my business. Before you knew it, that one tweet was liked over 100,000 times. I'd gone from 90 followers to a little over 12,000 in just two days. Having that many eyes on me was a little overwhelming because I'd always been someone who'd fall under the radar. I was never popular or the most social. I would handle my business and be in my world. So, this was different. However, at the same time, I embraced the attention because I was getting recognition for all the right reasons. I was being recognized for being a young black man who started his own successful business. I'll roll with that any day. While my business was growing and I started to grow a platform on social media, I also had a big change in my personal life. My girlfriend and I split for good. The split was very respectable. I agreed to leave her the apartment we shared and pay her bills. I felt it was important for her and our son to be taken care of and never have to worry about a roof over their head. If she's taken care of, then my son is taken care of. I went on to move into a one-bedroom apartment about 15 minutes away. I originally wanted to move into this luxury spot for about $800 more a month than what I was paying for my apartment, but I elected not to do so. I wasn't ready for that move just yet. I mean, yes, I was making more money, more money than I ever had before, but just because I made more didn't mean I needed to spend more. I had just started making some money. The last thing I wanted to do was start spending it all immediately. That's one thing people get wrong when they start to make money. They make more, so they spend more which, in theory, can make it seem like they're not making more. If you make $50,000 a month, but your expenses are $48,000 a month, what happens if you have a setback financially? We just witnessed a once-in-a-lifetime situation with the pandemic due to Covid-19. So, many people overleveraged themselves and found out the harsh realities that come with that. I'm not one to brag, but I must be honest, while I heard some people I know who were supposedly making all of this money talk about how they were struggling to pay their bills due to Covid-19, I was laid on my couch watching horror movie after horror movie on Netflix. That's because I subconsciously had been preparing for things like the pandemic for a while. I was saving my money because you never know, and I didn't want to waste money on a bunch of expensive designer clothes and shoes or splurge on a brand-new car. No, I was fine with the things I had. I'll do those things when I have what they call "F U" money. While I was in a relationship with my son's mother, she sold her old beat-up car, and we just shared mine. With the split, that was no longer possible, so I decided to give her my car and buy a car for myself. I had just come off of making $19,000 and $23,000 in back-to-back months, so of course, I had to splurge and get a nice car. I mean, I earned it, right? Wrong. I bought a 2008 Dodge Grand Caravan that had 67,000 miles on it. That van is what I was going to use to stock my vending machines. I didn't care about impressing anyone. This van would make me money, and when it wouldn't, I would use the van to get from point a to point b. One thing I learned while growing up poor was being able to focus on my needs over my wants. So, many times today, before I make a purchase, I'll ask myself, "Do you really need this?" The answer to that question is pretty much always no. So, most times, I wouldn't make the purchase. While some people who grew up in poverty like to splurge on the type of things they couldn't buy before they came across money, I felt like I made it this far without a pair of $800 shoes, so there's no point in buying them now. I've never gotten caught up in buying brand-name things. Listen, if I like it, I'll buy it. I don't care if the clothes are from Walmart. If I like it, I'll buy it. I've seen people spend $1,000 on their outfits and have to ask for a ride home because they don't have a car. Their priorities are not in order. Now I'm not going to pretend that I don't buy luxury stuff because I do. But I do it in moderation. I like to set a goal for myself if I'm looking to make a particularly expensive purchase. I've always wanted to purchase a Cuban link. I like jewelry, especially gold jewelry, so that's been on my things to-do list for a while. The Cuban link that I wanted to purchase cost between $6,500-7,500. I'd never made a purchase that large on something for myself before. I honestly stayed away from making purchases for me overall. I suffered from what you would call financial

PTSD. Due to growing up in poverty, I was scared to spend my money because I was fearful that I'd never make it back, so I was hoarding my money. I had to learn to enjoy my money. I knew that I wouldn't just start blowing money, but I did need to enjoy it, which is why I decided I'd only make an expensive purchase if I could set and achieve a financial goal. I had to set a high goal but not too high where I couldn't achieve it. So, I decided that I would pay for half of the Cuban link upfront and pay for the other half when I'd made $10,000 in sales from my various endeavors. It took me three weeks to reach that goal, and before you knew it, I bought my Cuban link. That set the standard for how I was going to make purchases moving forward. This is what works for me but I understand that it might not work for other people. Some people don't care and just want to splurge because they feel they got it. By all means, if that's your prerogative, go for it. Just understand that lack of discipline will catch up to you. It always does. Early on in life, I understood the value of money. I understand that money in itself was invaluable, but what it can do for you is where the value lies. I no longer have a dollar amount that I would like to earn that would make me feel successful. I want the amount that will allow me, together with my family, to be financially free. I try to acquire as many cash-flowing assets as I can because that is what's going to allow me to be financially free. When I started growing my vending machine business, I didn't think of becoming rich off of my vending machines. I thought about becoming free. If I earn $300 at a vending location, that would cover my car payment. That would cover my cell phone and internet bill. That's the mindset I have. I wanted to eliminate bills. I wanted to eliminate expenses, not add more. When my apartment lease was up, I wanted to move into downtown Philadelphia in this amazing penthouse. This penthouse is rented for $3,500 a month. I could more than afford it. But even though I liked the penthouse, I knew deep down I would've gotten it because it would've been a status move. It would've shown how successful I'd become. A kid from the westside of Rochester is now living in a penthouse in downtown Philadelphia. Sounds like such an amazing story. Can you imagine if I would've chosen to live in that penthouse instead of the apartment I moved into that cost less than half the amount, and I somehow lost my job? That's not hypothetical because that's what happened. I lost a behavior consultant contract that cost me $7,000-8,000 a month in income. Was I financially okay because of my investments and savings? Of course. Finding another was nothing to me, but I always think about what if? What if I had bought that expensive car to show people I had money? What if I had gotten that penthouse? What if I hadn't stuck to my principles? I'll never know because I'll never move off my principles. I will never forget to stack my money, acquire assets, not pocket watch, flex when necessary or act my wage. These five principles have guided me into becoming the successful man that I am today. I hope that they help guide you into becoming the successful person that you expect to become.

Acknowledgements:

I've been trying to write this book for over two years but couldn't find the motivation to do so until one night, I had a conversation with my friend Arielle. Thank you so much for encouraging me to write this book and giving me whatever resources I needed. Thank you to my siblings Rell, Kiesha, Mike, Matt, Larry, and Quazia. You all have always kept me grounded. Thank y'all, for pushing me to be better and want better. Nobody knows me as y'all know me. Most of all, I want to thank y'all for accepting that I'm the favorite. I know how difficult it may be. Just keep your chins up. Thank you, Yanique, who's one of the most loyal people I've ever met. Our conversation in March of 2018 is one I will always cherish. Thank you to my grandmother for all the support you've always given me. I wouldn't have been able to make it through my ACL surgery without you. Thank you to my Aunt Lou. I love you and miss you every day. I hope I've been able to make you proud. Thank you, grandad. You're one of my biggest inspirations. I wouldn't be the man I am without your guidance. You don't have to worry about the family anymore. I got it from here. Thank you, Pops. I wish words could express how much you mean to me. I could never pay you back for all you've done for me, so the best thing I can do is pay it forward. To my mother, thank you for always believing in me. You told me ever since I was a kid, I would be successful, and you meant it. Thank you for being there whenever I needed you. I'm proud of you, and I love you. Thank you, Kendal, not only for giving me an amazing son but for being an amazing mom. Thank you for the sacrifices you've made, which are some of the biggest reasons I am where I am today. I could never pay you back for what you've done, so I won't. It'll be too much money, and I'm not rich like that. Kameron and Kenneth, thank you for allowing me to be your dad. Everything I do, I do for you guys. No matter what I achieve or how successful I become, being your dad will always be my biggest accomplishment.

ACKNOWLEDGEMENTS

The ones that started it all. My first vending location.

The vending location that changed my life.

LAW OF INVESTING

My business branding.

The tweet that changed my life. From 90 followers on Twitter to 26,000 and counting.

ACKNOWLEDGEMENTS

Kenneth (on my lap) and Kameron. My two biggest inspirations.

Kameron stealing snacks instead of keeping inventory

Kenneth helping me pack snacks for the machines.

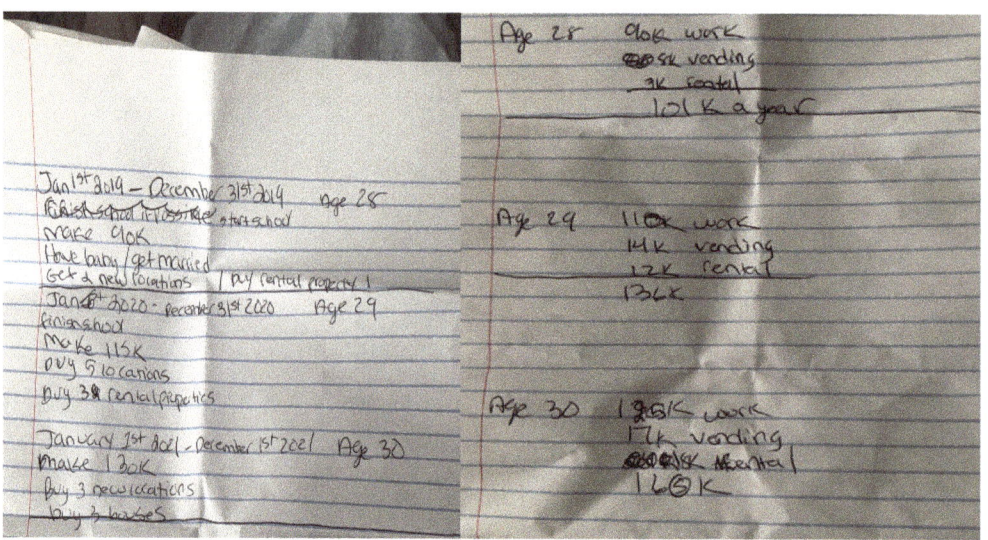

The different goals I wrote daily while working 3 pm-10 pm at my job.